Violence against Women

Why are women victims of violence by men?

What must be changed?

Violence against Women
Abuse in Society and Church and Proposals for Change

The Taskforce Report to General Synod 1986
of the Anglican Church of Canada

Anglican Book Centre
Toronto, Canada

1987
Anglican Book Centre
600 Jarvis Street
Toronto, Ontario
Canada M4Y 2J6

Typesetting by Jay Tee Graphics Ltd.

Canadian Cataloguing in Publication Data

Task Force of the Women's Unit of the Anglican Church
of Canada
   Violence against women

ISBN 0-919891-79-9

1. Women — Crimes against. 2. Violence. 3. Church
and social problems. I. Anglican Church of Canada.
General Synod. II. Title.

HV6250.4.W65T37 1987   362.8′3   C87-095258-7

Contents

**Taskforce on Violence against Women (1983–1986)
Anglican Church of Canada**

Ms. Pauline Bradbrook
Ms. Pat Clark
The Rev. John Flindall
The Rev. Janet Handy
Dr. Alan Hayes
The Rev. Cheryl Kristolaitis
Ms. Elizabeth Loweth
Ms. Kim Malcolmson
The Rev. Dr. James Reed
Ms. Jeanne Rowles
Professor Kathy Storrie
The Rev. Dr. Don Thompson
Ms. Elizabeth Wensley
The Rev. Maylanne Whittall

Preface

Violence in contemporary society takes many forms. None of them is more distressing than the physical and emotional abuse within the family relationship. It is only in recent years that Canadians have become aware of the extent to which women and children, and sometimes men, are subjected to such abuse. The shameful facts have been received with a mixture of disbelief, shock, anger, disgust, and (happily) a determination to understand the problem at greater depth and to take effective action to correct it.

The Anglican Church of Canada, through resolutions adopted by two successive sessions of the General Synod (1983 and 1986) has committed itself to a significant program of information gathering, consciousness raising, and carefully developed strategies designed to provide help in immediate crisis situations, and also to deal redemptively with the root causes of the problem.

The Taskforce on Violence against Women has provided this thought-provoking analysis of the issue, particularly in relation to wife battering. The General Synod of 1986 commended it for study and action, with special reference to the recommendations with which the report concludes. I gladly add my personal commendation to that of the General Synod, confident that all who are concerned about the church's ministry in today's all too violent society will find in the following pages much that is disturbing and therefore challenging, as well as suggestions for action in relation to one of the most troubling of current realities.

Archbishop Michael G. Peers,
Primate,
The Anglican Church of Canada.

Foreword

Wife abuse has reached endemic proportions in Western, post-industrial societies. It is the common lot of many women, a condition expected and accepted by many as "just the way things are." Women continue to be the most likely victims of abuse within adult, intimate relationships because we are the most vulnerable within those relationships. We are the most vulnerable because of the socialization and circumstance of patriarchy.

Whether through scripture, doctrine, custom, or legal mandate, patriarchy has granted males the prerogative to decide for others, to control others, to require of others, to chastise others. This patriarchal prerogative is the power to presume that females were created to serve the needs of men and the power to punish them when they do not. Men of colour or working class men who are denied this prerogative within the dominant culture nonetheless have retained it within their own race and class.

The persistence of the patriarchal prerogative compounds the problem of wife abuse. Many husbands still assume that they have the right to discipline their wives, the right to sex when they want it, the right to control their wive's activities, the right to have their needs serviced by women. The patriarchal prerogative is assumed as a birthright and serves to justify without question men's behaviour towards women.

If we are to comprehend the roots of wife abuse within patriarchy, we need a gender, race, and class analysis. When we rise up against the realities of racism, sexism, and classism, we can understand why women are the likely targets of abuse in intimate relationships and why violence works as the means chosen by an abuser to sustain his patriarchal prerogative.

If the church is to address wife assault, it must understand the patriarchal roots of the problem. If the church is to act, it must do so from a stance of confession. It must confess its collusion in the patriarchal prerogative. It must confess its role in prescribing abuse as fitting behaviour for husbands. It must confess its role in promulgating a theology which excuses wife battering. It must confess its silence through the centuries in the face of men's injustice towards women. It must confess its savage ignorance which has rendered it helpless to minister to women's suffering. Confessing, it must also repent of its role in sustaining the injustice of wife assault.

Cleansed by confession and repentance, the church is now ready to act, to minister in Christ's name with those who have been beaten, raped, and terrorized by their husbands. The church can act effectively when it calls upon a theology of liberation which takes seriously the experience of the vulnerable and abused and when it is willing to call to account those persons and institutions which perpetuate harm done to others. Then it will be empowered with courage and confidence to be the Good Samaritan in response to wife assault. Pray that it may be so.

This publication is an important contribution to our understanding of wife assault. Its candour and unequivocal analysis will greatly aid the church's task in fulfilling its mandate to bind up the wounded and set free those in bondage.

Marie M. Fortune,
Center for the Prevention
of Sexual and Domestic Violence

Introduction

The members of the Taskforce on Violence against Women, a taskforce of the Women's Unit of the Anglican Church of Canada, have cooperated in writing this paper. It was originally intended that the paper be written so that the taskforce members themselves could agree on a mutually acceptable statement of their analysis of woman battering. The taskforce, having worked on the issue for several years, asked itself: ''At this point, what do we understand to be the causes of woman battering?'' ''What have the roles of theology and of the church been in relation to woman battering?'' and ''What can we, as a part of the church, recommend that the church do to change the present situation?''

The paper is divided into three parts, each relating to one of these questions. The sections are

A The Structure of Society — Current Analyses
B Theological Reflection
C Response Strategies for the Church

In an appendix which sets out the Act of General Synod 1983 with respect to family violence, the taskforce makes specific recommendations for ways to work at implementing the act at every level of the church.

The taskforce found that the process of writing the report helped it to be clearer in its own analysis of violence against women. It now wishes to share the paper with other interested groups.

The report was accepted and endorsed by the Women's Unit at its October 1985 meeting. In February 1986, the Program Committee endorsed the report as ''an appropriate sociological and theological analysis of this issue in Canadian society, and as a timely agenda for action by the church,'' and agreed to include it in the Program Committee report to General Synod 1986. General Synod, 1986, acted upon the report as follows:

That General Synod:

i   commend the report of the Taskforce on Violence against Women for study and action, with particular reference to recommendations 1-6 of the report [see appendix];

ii encourage dioceses

    a   to provide the resources necessary to implement the recommendations of the report of the Taskforce on Violence against Women;

    b   to report progress and suggestions to the Women's Unit for forwarding to the National Executive Council through the Program Committee prior to the 1989 General Synod;

iii request the Committee on Ministry:

    a   to bring the report of the Taskforce on Violence against Women to the attention of all Anglican centres of theological education in Canada with particular reference to the implications contained within the report for theological education; and

    b   to request those centres to implement the appropriate recommendations and response strategies of the report.

The motion as amended was put and *carried in all orders.*

Act 35

The Structure of Society — Current Analyses

1 Why focus on wife battering?

Violence against women takes a number of forms and occurs in different social contexts. The marital relationship constitutes one such context and this paper focuses on wife assault as one example of the abuse inflicted on women. Wife assault merits the fullest attention of Anglicans, and indeed of Christians in general, for a number of reasons.

First of all, many Christians remain unaware of the extent to which the church has been implicated in condoning and even supporting the behaviour of husbands when they physically punished their wives. Indeed, the church defined such "discipline" as the bounden duty of a husband in order to correct his wife's soul (see, e.g. Fortune, 1982; Dobash and Dobash, 1979).

A second reason Christians should take pains to confront this particular form of abuse is that theological legitimization has served to reinforce other cultural rationalizations, such as "A man's home is his castle," so that wife battering has been trivialized and rendered invisible. In focusing on wife abuse, we do not minimize other forms of intimate violence and abuse, such as the abuse of children. Yet for decades social institutions have recognized and have named child abuse for what it is. Much more remains to be done, particularly in the case of sexual abuse of children, but at least child abuse is now widely recognized by the state and the helping professions, whereas assaults on wives still tend to be denied and disguised. To cite just one example of the difference in the official response to these two types of behaviour, all the provinces now have a central registry in which all cases of reported child abuse are recorded, but no such registry exists anywhere in Canada for women.

A third reason for a focus on wife battering is its widespread and frequent occurrence. For example, in an analysis of cases of violence reported in two Scottish cities in 1974, assaults against wives were the second most common violent offense. Further, a third of the cases involved family members and, of these, 78% consisted of husbands assaulting their wives (Dobash and Dobash, 1979). A Canadian report estimates that 10% of Canadian women who are married or in a common-law relationship are battered (MacLeod, 1980), but this statistic probably under-represents the real situation.

All the evidence supports the conclusion that physical force between husbands and wives is systematically directed at women. While it is true that some husbands are beaten by their wives, these constitute a very small proportion of cases (1.1% in Dobash and Dobash's Scottish study), and in most of them the women are reacting to the initial violence of their husbands. Interviews with a representative sample of American households through the National Crime Survey in the United States revealed that although men have a far greater risk of being physically assaulted than do women, they have almost no risk of being assaulted by their wives, whereas almost 15% of all assaults against women are perpetrated by their husbands or ex-husbands (Gaguin, 1978). Furthermore, such assaults, compared to other types of assaults, are more likely to result in injury, to require medical attention and hospitalization, and to result in time lost from work.

Even when it is the woman alone who is being violent, such behaviour on the part of women has never been condoned institutionally — that is by custom, by law, by the state, and by the church — whereas the assault of women by their husbands has been so supported. Our position, then, is that while violence by either gender must be condemned, our first task as a church is to unmask and confront systemic evil.

2 Mutually reinforcing hierarchies

The injunction that a man should physically punish his wife to correct her soul illustrates just one way in which the church has been implicated in providing structural support for wife abuse (see section 6. Ideological aspects). The church has not been alone in providing such support. Government, the legal system, and other social systems have behaved in a similar manner — as mutually reinforcing hierarchies which produce and maintain both class and gender inequalities.

As we will see, domestic labour — the labour of wives — is an arena where the hierarchies of patriarchy and capitalism meet. Historically, the church and the state gave husbands the right to "discipline" their wives, and capitalism built on this subordination by defining the wife's domestic labour as a "personal service" which she owes to her husband in return for being his dependent. The church has supported the economic system in obtaining free use of women's labour.* In this first section of the paper, which deals with the structure of our society, we will examine the family farm, and working class and middle class homes. In each case, the unpaid work of the wife is shaped differently by the occupational position of the husband, but in all

---

*For example, as mentioned later (see section 10. Domestic ideology and female submission), in the late eighteenth and early nineteenth century, the Clapham Sect, an influential group of Anglican evangelicals, contributed significantly to a new emphasis on women as primarily *domestic* beings, subordinate to their husbands. The life's work of a woman was redefined: it was to be devoted solely to management of the home, support and care of the husband, child bearing and child rearing, and sustaining (even improving) male morality. (Some philanthropic work outside the home was encouraged). Although this "cult of true womanhood" was religiously motivated, it laid the foundation for a secular bourgeois ideal of the family that became culturally exalted, i.e. married women should not "work outside the home." In this way, the church, in effect, promoted and legitimated the appropriation of female domestic labour not only by husbands but also by capitalism, since this unpaid labour was crucial in re-creating and replenishing the labour power of male workers within the haven of the home. (See, e.g. Catherine Hall, "The Early Formation of Victorian Domestic Ideology," in S. Burman, ed., *Fit Work for Women*, London: Croom Helm, 1979.)

of them a wife is in a vulnerable position because her work is both essential for her husband's paid work and unrecognized as such. Instead, her work is usually seen as her "wifely duty" — an effective disguise for the husband's emotional and physical dependence on her.

We will also look at this dependence — which arises in part from the fact that the wife is expected to relieve her husband's tensions even though their origins lie beyond her control. The tension-management role is accentuated by stereotyped notions of masculinity, whereby the expression of certain emotions is regarded as "unmanly" while rage and physical aggression are not. In so far as a man believes he should be dominant over his wife and that it is permissible to use violence within marriage, and to the degree that he cannot express the full range of his feelings, his wife is in danger of being assaulted.

3 Woman as victim

Wife abuse is best understood in terms of two aspects: violence directed against women as women and against women as wives. The first aspect involves women's gender, i.e. their identity which is socially constructed, and the second aspect involves their role as wives. In this way, wife abuse can be viewed in the wider context of violence against women, of "woman" as the appropriate victim.

An analysis of literature from 17 different disciplines throws some light on "woman" as the appropriate victim. The two psychologists who undertook this review concluded that "for aggression to be chosen as a response and for women to be chosen as a target of this aggression, there has to be a climate in which asymmetrical sex roles are adopted and the female devalued" (Stark-Adamec and Adamec, 1982, p. 17). "Asymmetrical sex roles" refer to disparities in such things as power, privilege, and prestige between women and men.

These findings are supported by a recent study of rape in which the authors argue that the general level of violence in a given society, including violence against women, is related to social arrangements which have a higher degree of sexual inequality (Schewendinger and Schewendinger, 1983). Another way of stating this is to say that male supremacy, an exploitative economy, and violence against women combine in different forms in different cultures and at different historical periods.

Male supremacy in capitalist societies is based on male monopoly over female labour, both paid and unpaid, and on patriarchal values originating from pre-capitalist institutions such as the church. Obviously violence against women predates capitalism, but capitalist conditions tend to produce character structures in men which are aligned with their experience of exploitative relations in their employment. Furthermore, violence and male dominance form basic components of the stereotyped image of masculinity, particularly in its portrayal in the mass media.

4 The wife as victim

Many people assume that violence always indicates a breakdown in the social order which the state and other institutions will try to diminish. However, until very recently, this is precisely what has not happened in the case of violence against wives. How can this be explained?

We need to understand that under certain conditions violence may be a purposeful means of social control which is socially condoned. Violence may serve to support rather than to disrupt a particular set of relations, and it may be in the interests of the state and the church to turn a blind eye in its direction as long as it does not disrupt other relations, especially public ones. Violent acts and interactions do not make sense when viewed in isolation. Since wife assault occurs in the home and in terms of a marital relationship, we need to examine this setting and this relationship. We take the position, then, that we can best understand wife assault, and society's response to it, in terms of the context of marriage and the work done in the home, primarily by women, namely domestic labour.

5 Domestic labour

''Domestic labour'' refers to the daily domestic work which provides for the survival and refreshment of the members of the household as well as for the actual producing of the next generation. This work includes child-bearing, child-care, husband-care, housework, "making ends meet" (budgeting, shopping, etc.), overall running and coordination of the household, "kinkeeping" (e.g. remembering birthdays and anniversaries), and a myriad of other activities. There is overwhelming evidence that it is still women who do most of this work, and those married women who are employed typically carry a "double load," that is a paid job and their domestic labour (see, e.g., Luxton, 1980; Meissner et al., 1975; Fox, 1980; Raimondi, 1983). Domestic labour constitutes both the context in which wives are beaten by their husbands and the basis of female dependency, which in turn helps to make it difficult for wives to escape from their husbands' violence.

Historically both the church and the state gave husbands the absolute right to appropriate and control, if necessary by force, the personal services of their wives, which included sexual services (Dobash and Dobash, 1979; Bauer and Ritt, 1983; Gage, 1893, reprinted in 1980). In Canada husbands could rape their wives with complete legal impunity until 1982, when the Criminal Code was changed. It is this context of institutional support which led Dobash and Dobash to state, "The use of physical force against wives should be seen as an attempt on the part of the husband to bring about a desired state of affairs. It is primarily purposeful behaviour and not the action of deviant or aberrant individuals or the prerogative of deviant or unusual families" (1979, p. 24).

Violence against wives thus arises, in part, from social hierarchies (chains of command), one of which is patriarchy, a system of power and privilege in which men are ranked above women.

6 Ideological aspects

One of the roots of our cultural legacy of patriarchy can be found in the early Roman Empire in which the family was one of the strongest patriarchies known. Its male head was priest, magistrate, and owner of all properties, which included all family members. The power of the patriarch extended to the right to put a wife or child to death without recourse to public trial. It was the case, then as now, that law makers and public officials preferred not to intervene in domestic affairs, but fully supported the husband in his enforcement of his absolute domination of his wife.*

By the time Christianity emerged, the status of wives in the Roman Empire had improved to some extent. However, it was not these reforms but the earlier Roman traditions of female sub-jugation which were eventually incorporated into church law. Canon law, in turn, infiltrated Anglo-Saxon law despite its egalitarian traditions (Gage, 1893, reprinted 1980). The canon law set the general principles of gender relations that guided the laws of all Europe. These principles excluded wives from legal pro-cess, defining them as property and placing them alongside ser-vants and children. Both the church and the state gave husbands a legal right to inflict corporal punishment which was effectively unrestricted. There were some laws which specified the ''mis-demeanours'' for which the wife could be beaten severely with whips and clubs and those for which only ''moderate correction'' would be appropriate (Dobash and Dobash, 1979).

A fifteenth century church publication called ''Rules of Mar-riage'' includes the following statement:

> Scold your wife sharply, bully and terrify her. If this does not work, take up a stick and beat her soundly, for it is better to punish the body and correct the soul than to damage the soul and spare the body. . . . Then readily beat her, not in rage but out of charity and concern for her soul, so that the beating will redound to your merit and her good. (Fortune, 1982, p. 19)

---

*In early Roman and Greek societies, the household was defined as a ''private sphere,'' over which the male head of the family could rule with impunity. (See, e.g., Elshtain, Jean, *Public Man, Private Woman: Women in Social and Political Thought*, Princeton: Princeton University Press, 1981, p. 3.) This public/private split became institutionalized in Western culture generally. It reinforced masculine hegemony in several ways — for example, it constituted an important ideological barrier to state intervention in domestic violence that has continued to this day. The generally ineffectual response of the criminal justice system to so-called ''domestic disputes'' has been very well-documented. (See, e.g., MacLeod, 1980; Roy, 1982; Walker, 1979.)

In some instances canon law exacted more severe punishment than the old Roman law. For example, the latter prohibited burning alive as being too barbarous, but the church did not, with respect to women. (Men were usually strangled before their bodies were burned.) This provision was put to full use during the reign of terror sponsored by the church and known as the witch-hunts. Eighty-five % of those burned were women (Dobash and Dobash, 1979).

This discussion of the influence of patriarchy on church law and practice is not intended to deny the existence of another tradition within Christianity which was much more sympathetic to women and indeed to all "lesser ones" (those of low social status). The most striking example of this can be found in the egalitarian stance of Jesus himself. He went out of his way to affirm women as fully persons and equal partners with men (see, for example, Swidler, 1979; Fiorenza, 1983). However, most church historians agree that eventually this egalitarian tradition became very much a minor theme in the history of the church, at least until more recent times (Tavard, 1973).

Thus it is not surprising that it was the state and not the institutional church which took the lead in undermining and finally eliminating the husband's legal right to "chastise" his wife. This did not occur until the nineteenth century, and only then was it achieved after long, arduous struggles. These began with the work of such individuals as Mary Wollstonecraft and John Stuart Mill in England, and of the women's emancipation movements on both sides of the Atlantic. These movements fought vigorously against wife assault, and their analysis was very similar to that of the contemporary movement (see, for example, Bauer and Ritt, 1983).

Removing the statutes did not, of course, eliminate the violence nor the reluctance of the church and state to breach in any way what was thought of as "the sanctity" of marriage and home, through effective intervention. More will be said about this later, but to cite just one example of this reluctance, cruelty only became grounds for divorce in Canada in 1968. Prior to that, a wife had to prove that abuse caused her "danger in life, limb, physical and mental health." An Ontario Chief Justice commented in 1920:

A man may subject his wife, daily and even hourly, to such treatment as makes her life a veritable hell on earth, and she is without remedy, if she is robust enough to suffer it without impairment of her physical health or her mentality.

In this country, it was the much maligned Women's Movement which took up the cause of abused women and not the "official" institutions, whether religious or secular.

7 Patriarchy and capitalism

Canada, like other Western nations, is a class society, so another "chain of command" has been created by its economic system. The social location of wife assault, the home, is profoundly influenced by capitalist relations, and it is here that capitalism and patriarchy interact — in and through the daily domestic work of women.

One of the most important aspects of domestic labour is that of tension management — a responsibility which wives have regardless of class, although the particular context may vary according to the husband's occupation. The woman is expected to maintain the home as a "sanctuary," showing the outside world an image of peace and tranquility, where members of the family, and particularly the husband, are soothed and replenished. In this way, the family members are enabled to return to the struggles of the world of school or employment (Luxton, 1980; Smith, 1977). It is the women's role as tension managers that makes them logical victims of domestic violence, given the definition of their domestic work as "personal services" produced in exchange for their husbands' financial support, and given the authority which the state and the church have bestowed upon husbands to control wives and children.

Killoran points out that

in its crudest formulation, wife abuse may be seen as an extreme form of tension-management — the woman absorbs with her psyche and her body the tensions generated in the public sphere. . . . this can be seen as "functional" for a capitalist economy which requires that workers internalize a hierarchical view of relationships and at the same time that they not vent their frustration on the job. (1982, p. 10)

Furthermore, the wife must also absorb those tensions that may arise as a result of any discrepancy between her own expectations of her role as wife-and-mother and those of the man she lives with. If she does not meet those expectations, then her behaviour may well be defined by her husband, and indeed by others, as "provocative." This definition, though, is based on the assumption that the husband has the right to control his wife. She is seen as having no real rights to resources such as time, money, or mobility, although she may negotiate for them as long as her husband does not object to her doing so.

8 Canadian contexts

For the purpose of this discussion, we will focus briefly on three situations in which the domestic labour of women and their dependency on their husbands are differently shaped by capitalist/patriarchal relations. These are the situations of farm women, working-class women, and middle-class women. We identify only some of the salient features in each by way of illustrating the different contexts in which wife abuse occurs in Canada.

a   Farm wives

The beating of farm wives needs to be viewed in the context of the husband's being constituted as economic agent, appropriating his wife's labour as part of the farm enterprise. The domestic and farm economies she can achieve continue to be as essential as in earlier times, yet the farm as an economic unit is still organized on the traditional, patriarchal principle of being rooted in the person of her husband.

Until recent changes in matrimonial law (and these vary among provinces), the wife had no guarantee at all of any share in the property and assets in the event of marriage break-up. In many provinces her share is still subject to considerable judicial discretion. In some provinces, such as Saskatchewan, the changed matrimonial law is being bitterly disputed by many male farmers who strongly support exclusive male ownership of property. What is specifically in dispute is whether a wife's domestic and farm work should be counted as having direct economic value to the viability of the farm, or whether it should revert to its former status of constituting merely her "wifely duty" — that is, as something to be appropriated by her husband as rightfully his. If her labour is his by right, then it cannot be counted as hers and as her economic contribution to the business. It was precisely this "wifely duty" or "personal service" principle which became well publicized in such cases as Rathwell and Murdoch. Neither the field work nor the domestic work of these women provided any legal basis for their access to any farm assets at separation and divorce under the matrimonial laws of Saskatchewan and Alberta respectively.*

Access to off-farm employment for women has become increasingly difficult, so that financial dependency, combined with isolation and a lack of "safe homes" and other services in rural areas, renders the situation of the battered farm wife particularly dangerous and difficult. Furthermore, the continued price/costs squeeze is raising emotional tensions on farms to even higher levels — tensions which farm wives must try to defuse, sometimes at their peril.

*The Rathwell case occurred in Saskatchewan and the Murdoch one took place in Alberta in the nineteen seventies. In the words of the Saskatchewan Advisory Council on the Status of Women: "In both situations the marriages had been of lengthy duration, the women had made significant contributions of labour to the value and expansion of the properties — a large ranch in [the] Murdoch [case], a large farm in [the] Rathwell [case]. Both women sought a share in the wealth of the property when the marriage broke down. In both cases the courts refused to recognize any such rights for the women and each was awarded simply a small sum of maintenance" (*Report on Matrimonial Property Legislation*, 1983, p. 3). (Rathwell was awarded, eventually, a portion of the property by the Supreme Court of Canada). There had been similar cases previously but what was new was the degree of public demand for the reform of matrimonial property legislation — a demand led by feminist groups and organizations that has brought about legislative changes in most of the provinces.

Furthermore, the domestic labour of a farm wife is unique, in that without her the family farm as a unit cannot continue to exist, either in the present or in the future, as an inheritance for the next generation. From this perspective, one can see that practically everything a farm wife does relates to two vitally important matters — the ongoing economic viability of the farm and the producing and rearing of an heir, who, needless to say, must typically be a son. All this is not to suggest that male farmers are somehow more prone than other men to beat their wives, but rather to point to the fact that the inequality of farm wives continues to be structured institutionally, specifically in terms of male property rights. These include the right to the work of the wife. Under these conditions, patriarchal notions are bound to appear particularly right and "normal," and for some male farmers they do include the supposed right of husbands to "discipline" their wives.

The case of Jeannie Fox — an abused farm wife

Jeannie's story is recounted in the National Film Board film, *Love, Honoured and Bruised*. In a NFB pamphlet about the film, Johanna Brand states:

> Jeannie was married 16 years to a man who physically and mentally abused her. The first two years of her married life were normal. It was only after the birth of their first child that the violence started. When the baby [a girl] was six months old, Jeannie's husband threw a teapot of freshly brewed tea at them. Four children and thirteen years later, she left him. (NFB, p. 1)

In addition to her domestic labour, Jeannie worked hard at many farm tasks since no hired help could be afforded. But in the film she labels this work as "helping" her husband. The final attack included a partial strangulation and a ruptured eardrum inflicted by a box to her head. Just prior to this, Jeannie tried to anticipate her husband's every wish as she worked in a vain effort to stave off his savagery. He threatened to kill her if she did not go and take with her those "useless, squalling brats." Although it is not stated explicitly, it seems probable that one of the reasons Jeannie's husband beat her was that none of the children was a son.

The film illustrates well the isolation and vulnerability of abused farm women. For example, in their flight, Jeannie and her daughters faced a five-mile walk to the nearest town. Fortunately a woman neighbour picked them up in her truck and took them to the nearest RCMP station. It turned out that she had known for some time about the beatings and had been watching the Fox farm that morning.

The husband is interviewed on camera and acknowledges the unfairness of venting his frustrations on his wife. But he fails to recognize his violence. "I am a timid sort," he says. "He seems incapable of appreciating the full impact of his behaviour towards his family despite the fact that they had to flee for their personal safety" (Brand, p. 2). At one point he compares his treatment of his wife to having to discipline a child. "You do it because you love them," he says.

After staying in Osbourne House, a shelter in Winnipeg, Jeannie has been able to obtain a separation and to start a new life with her children.

b Working-class wives
The beating of wives by working-class men is also linked to a property relation — in this case, the power of the wage earner who is also the wage owner. Historically, it was in the interests of the state, capitalists, and the trade unions to constitute the ideal of the husband as the only wage-earner, with the wife and children as his dependents. This ideal formed part of the trade union strategy to combat the threat to the male wage posed by the lower bargaining power of women (and children) in the nineteenth century (Hartman, 1984). Indeed, the struggle to achieve an adequate "family wage" with good working conditions and pensions, etc., for skilled blue-collar male workers went hand-in-hand with the systematic exclusion of women from the skilled sector of the labour force and their relegation to the "marginal" market, i.e. to dead-end and badly paid jobs.

To cite only a few cases out of the mass of evidence supporting this point. Research into the British printing industry in the nineteenth century found a "constant and vigilant opposition of Trade Unions to the employment and technical training of women in better paid and more skilled branches of trade" (Fawcett, 1904), and the same processes occurred in U.S. industry. For example, the International Molders Union resolved, "Any member . . . who devotes his time to the instruction of female help in the foundry or in any branch of the trade shall be expelled from the Union" (Falk, 1970). Similarly, a local of the Cigar-makers International Union in 1878 rejoiced in the fact that they had "combatted from its incipiency the movement of the introduction of female labour in any capacity whatsoever" (Baker, 1964, p. 34).

The net effect has been to increase the economic power of the working-class husband over his wife and simultaneously to bind him to his job, however much he may hate it. In Luxton's words: "From her position of economic dependency, a wife adds more pressure to the structural compulsion on men to work" (1980, p. 66).

In this way, capitalism and patriarchal ideology have combined to find working-class masculinity on a highly precarious base, since the individual man has no control over the conditions of his wage-earning capacity. This uncertainty makes his visible dominance over his wife and children all the more important, and given the historical sanctioning of physical force as a means of asserting male control over dependents, it is not surprising that wife abuse occurs frequently. Furthermore, blue-collar men are often placed in powerless, alienating, and humiliating situations. Inevitably they bring considerable bottled-up anger home. Wives are sometimes literally "stand-ins" for a hated boss or supervisor, as Luxton documents in her study of Flin Flon, Manitoba.

In one case, a male worker who fought regularly with his supervisor would get drunk or stoned on marijuana regularly after work at night. He would lash out at his wife:

> Once he came at me with the kitchen knife saying I was [the boss] and he wasn't going to take no more shit from me. Another time, he took a swipe at me and broke my glasses. (Luxton, p. 69)

Another woman who was beaten regularly by her husband was recovering after a particularly bad attack in which her arm was broken. Luxton comments that what she said explains, in part, why so many women accept the abuse they receive from their husbands:

He puts up with shit every day at work and he only works because he has me and the kids to support. Weren't for us he'd be off trapping on his own, with no boss breathing down his neck. He hates his job. He's got all that mad locked up inside with nowhere for it to go. So sometimes he takes it out on me and the kids. Well, I sort of don't blame him I guess. (p. 70)

Luxton goes on to point out:

Thus a terrible but logical and extreme extension of their roles as tension managers is for women, as the victim, to blame themselves and to feel guilty for having induced male hostility and aggression. (p. 70)

c Middle-class wives

The middle- or upper-class marriage differs in many ways from its nineteenth-century form in which continuities of property and the consolidation of capital across generations depended on a patriarchal set of relations (see, e.g., the *Forsythe Saga* by John Galsworthy.) These relations subsumed the wife as a civil person under the person of her husband so that he appropriated her property and earnings as well as her domestic labour. It was only when the alternative institutions for consolidating and transmitting capital such as corporations, trusts, etc., were developed and firmly in place, that the male elite permitted modest legal changes to be enacted which permitted wives to hold property of their own and to retain their own earnings. These changes in marital property laws occurred in Canada between 1915 and 1924 (excluding Quebec) (Smith, 1980). Women were not granted the legal status of "persons" in Canada until 1929 (Eberts, 1979).

As the ownership of the means of production shifted to the corporate rather than individual form of ownership, the work of the middle-class wife became focused on supporting and advancing her husband's career within a professional or bureaucratic hierarchy. These expectations have continued into this century. Furthermore, the wife is expected to produce a home, a household, and children that demonstrate a physical and moral image appropriate to an external moral order — that defined by the corporation or bureaucracy (see, e.g., Seeley et al, 1963).

In this sense, the wife becomes an agent of the corporate enterprise or profession. The "traditional" role of the clergy wife is an obvious case in point here (Finch, 1983). The middle-class wife shares this incorporation into her husband's work with farm and other women. However, the emphasis on her role as "the angel of the home," whether in its nineteenth-century or modern dress (a la Marabel Morgan's "Total Woman"), is particularly a middle- and upper-class phenomenon. Furthermore, her tension management capacities and other wifely competencies even today become matters for public scrutiny when her husband is being considered for a new job or a promotion. This is not so likely to occur in a blue-collar situation unless the prospective job has unusual conditions such as a geographically isolated location. Like other women, the middle-class wife is liable to be caught in a contradictory and potentially perilous position, in that her support of her husband's role in his job may be taken by him on occasion to imply support of the very system which may be violating him (Smith, 1977).

A middle-class wife may have more resources than a working-class wife in terms of education and possibly a reasonably well-paying job, but obviously middle-class wives vary in these respects. However, an abused middle-class wife may have more difficulty than a lower-income woman in admitting to and disclosing her husband's beatings. This is because of the emphasis which is placed on her respectability in her social circles, and the incredulity with which any disclosure of the husband's beatings may be greeted, especially if he is a "pillar" of the community and/or church. In addition, public knowledge of his violence may have negative implications for his reputation or even his job, or at least his wife may fear these repercussions. Alternatively, the husband may use the threat of such repercussions in order to silence her or to prevent her leaving.

In a study of battered middle-class women, Davidson points out that they have more to lose through disclosure than lower-income women in status, possessions, standard of living, and ego loss. Davidson comments:

This woman is shattered by the shock of "lower-class type" behaviour appearing in her marriage. There is such a taboo in her world against taking a husband to court or calling the police because of him or even admitting the barbarisms, that she has fewer options for relief. And she is aghast at the thought of going on welfare. (1978, p. 70)

Terry Davidson's story
The following is an excerpt from Terry Davidson's book *Conjugal Crime:*

> I know firsthand about the problem: I grew up with it. I was the unwilling witness to my father's habitual violence toward my mother. My father, ironically, was a member of one of those professions to which battered wives often first turn for help. He was a clergyman.
>
> I grew up in fear of that wifebeater's power, despising what was going on inside the parsonage. It was made very clear that I must keep silent about my father's predilection. . . . My instinct was to scream for help from the very beginning, but there was no help then. His wifebeating was the family secret, the family skeleton, decreed by both mother and father never to be let out of the closet. Divorce was a sin — and so was exposing my father's conjugal crime.
>
> Although I tried, I never was in a position to aid my battered mother effectively, and my outrage at the continuing injustice and the apparent do-nothingness of the community would not go away. As long as my parents lived, my belief — mistaken, I now realize — that somehow sanity and the Christian ethic would prevail, was never entirely extinguished.

Terry Davidson's experience as the daughter of a clergy wife-beater motivated her to do a wide-ranging study of middle-class wife abuse. She ends her book on a note of hope:

> Once there is awareness, many good people in many communities will be ready to listen, understand at last and help. There need never again be another family like the one in the parsonage. (p. 160)

pastoral issues

9 Domestic hierarchy, tension management, and control of wives

In order to understand wife assault more fully, we need to explore the tension management role of wives from the point of view of husbands. As we have seen, paid labour for many men is often an alienating, hurtful experience; yet it is not in the interests of patriarchal capitalism for such feelings to be expressed and dealt with on the job, or for them to be translated into political action such as union activity. Through the ideology of the "masculine mystique," patriarchal capitalism teaches men to repress many of their feelings, particularly those arising out of being a subordinate in a chain of command on the job. These feelings include self-doubt, fear, anxiety, shame, and longings for affection and emotional support. This learning begins at an early age and is reinforced by the media, language patterns, the schools, etc., so that many men do not know how to express these feelings. In fact, they may have trouble in being able to identify these feelings for what they are.

Chains of command have another effect. We need to notice that a typical practice of superiors in a hierarchy is to blame subordinates for any discomfort or problems which they (the superiors) may be experiencing. This is specially true of domestic hierarchy in which men expect their wives to meet all their emotional, as well as physical and sexual needs.

One member of Emerge — a program for abusive men in Boston — has said:

> My wife was there to make me feel good. "Why didn't you fix my supper the way I wanted it?" That sort of thing. In any number of ways that was her primary role I think — feeding me, nourishing me emotionally. And after a period of time, I became very inept at nourishing myself. (Roy, 1982, p. 178).

Abusive men typically lack emotional skills. They tend to fuse any or all repressed feelings onto the one emotion which they are comfortable accepting in themselves and expressing — namely rage (Fortune and Hormann, 1980). In addition, their expectations of the tension management capacities of their wives can be stated characteristically as: "She should know what I want when I want it and I shouldn't have to tell her" (Fortune and Hormann, 1980, p. 57).

Inevitably, a wife cannot possibly meet such unrealistic demands; the man explodes into violence; his sense of discomfort disappears; he has re-asserted control over the supposed cause of his problems — his wife. His rage is often replaced by remorse and contrite behaviour which may last until the tension builds up again and the cycle is repeated, with an escalating level of violence (Walker, 1979). Not surprisingly, most abusive men are extremely jealous and possessive of their wives, being willing to do anything to keep them, including killing or maiming them. Such husbands often set up a surveillance system whereby they control and monitor their wives' every activity. This analysis is amply supported by the evidence of abusive husbands themselves, men who have been through successful group treatment programs (Adams and McCormick, 1982), and of abused wives (Roy, 1982).

Before leaving this question of how the organization of emotions in men is linked to both economic and domestic hierarchies, we need to notice how useful this pattern is for the economic system and for the state. It encourages men to externalize their problems, to deflect their rage onto intimates, their wives. Wives make convenient scapegoats because they are isolated in their homes and are unorganized as a group and therefore politically powerless. Furthermore, wives' tension-management role allows husbands and the community in general to hold them accountable for everything occurring in the home, including their husbands' violence. The women have also been taught to hold themselves responsible in this way.

In abused wives, this conditioning process is taken much deeper, to a level which Lenore Walker has diagnosed as a state known to psychologists as "learned helplessness." This phrase refers to a psychological state in which persons or animals have been conditioned to believe that they are powerless to influence the outcome of events which are affecting them. That is, they believe that no response on their part will change their situation. As a result, they adopt submissive, self-blaming, and denying techniques in order to survive. Walker comments:

This concept [of learned helplessness] is important for understanding why battered women sometimes do not attempt to gain their freedom from a battering relationship. They do not believe they can escape from the batterer's domination. Often their perceptions are accurate but they need not be for this theory to work. (1979)

Thus the psychic injuries men sustain in the public realm are contained within the private realm. The anger aroused by these injuries is safely defused onto the bodies and souls of women and children — safely from the state's point of view. (Only 20% of men who batter their wives are violent in other situations). Such a policy of containment supports the view presented earlier that violence is not necessarily disruptive of the general social order. Indeed, privatized violence is a very effective means of social control.

For this system to be maintained, however, assaults on wives must be made invisible, by being minimized and defined as something else through ideological practices. These practices can be understood by seeing them as "interested procedures which people use as a means not to know" (Smith, 1974, p. 10).

For example, in the case of the police and the criminal justice system in general these "interested" procedures include defining wife beatings as "domestic disputes," i.e. as non-criminal because of the marital relationships involved; defining the household as private and therefore outside "ordinary" policing; and evoking "the sanctity of the family" (Storrie, 1985). An Ontario report has stated:

The police officer's attitudes reflect society's belief that the family is a sacrosanct unit. . . . (Ontario, Standing Committee on Social Development, 1983)

What is meant by "the family" in police work? A close scrutiny reveals that the term refers to the traditional concept of a dominant husband who is the sole breadwinner and a wife who devotes herself to full-time domestic labour.

10 Domestic ideology and female submission

Such a domestic ideology owes much, of course, to the doctrines and practices of the church. Indeed the Church of England, through the Clapham Sect in the nineteenth century, played a central role in promoting "the cult of true womanhood" in which male dominance and female submission were systematically elevated as cardinal Christian virtues (Hall, 1979; Ruether, 1973; Storrie, 1983).

The doctrine of female submission has received fresh support since the 1960s through a widespread movement involving many denominations (Storrie, 1983). Many Christians continue to believe that the Bible teaches sexual hierarchy, and some also teach that wives should submit to their husbands under all conditions, including violence. Clergy and lay persons of this persuasion are likely to tell a battered wife that her abusive husband is "her cross" and that she must bear it. For example, Bill Gothard, of the Institute in Basic Youth Conflicts, argues that by submitting to abusive husbands women learn "to suffer for righteousness' sake." In 1982, 330,000 people went to the Gothard Seminars in the United States and Canada.

Furthermore, a recent study of pastors' response to wife abuse has found that pastors who distrust and minimize a woman's report of spousal abuse "will also be significantly inclined to require that she submit to her violent husband" (Alsdurf, 1985, p. 10). Also the study showed that "pastors who endorse a wife's submission to her husband and to God in the face of violence do not support a woman's efforts to protect herself from a violent husband (through legal intervention and protection)."

11 Economic dependence of wives

Yet another link in the chain which binds many women to abusive husbands consists of women's disadvantage in the labour market. The concentration of women in a job ghetto of clerical work, sales, services, health, and teaching has increased from 71% in 1971 to

74% in 1981. In 1981, women with university degrees, on average, earned as much as men with only some high-school education (Women's Bureau, 1984). Women employed full-time averaged 64% of men's full-time earnings, and women employed part-time earned 63% of the wages of their male counterparts (National Council of Welfare, 1985). Most employed women work in the "marginal" labour market, i.e. in dead-end and badly paid jobs. Women make up 60.5% of the total labour force employed in the services sector; and workers in that sector (as compared to all other occupational groups) have the second highest risk of poverty (20.7%) next to those in farming and fishing (22.9%) (N.C.W. 1985).

The reasons for the occupational inequality between women and men are numerous, but one major factor is women's onerous role in domestic labour. This leads to their being defined as economic dependents of men and as "secondary" earners who can supposedly be paid less than men (who are defined as "primary" earners) even when they are doing similar work (Women's Bureau, 1984). Furthermore, housework and childcare responsibilities often limit the occupational and educational options of women. This is particularly true if good and affordable child care is not available, and frequently it is not. Stereotyping and prejudice provide further barriers, especially to the entry of women into skilled, well-paid jobs such as the blue-collar trades.

Not surprisingly, single-parent women are highly vulnerable to poverty. Fifty percent of them were poor in 1983 as compared to 11% of couples with children (N.C.W. 1985). Thus the economic outlook for most women who do leave abusive men is bleak indeed. Many face a bitter choice between abuse and poverty.

In summary, female vulnerability to male violence in intimate relations is heightened by ideological practices which minimize such violence, render it invisible, and blame the victim. Historically, the church has had a central part in generating and maintaining such practices, and continues to do so to the degree that its present theology and structures support sexual inequality. The next section of this paper is a theological reflection which leads to suggestions on how theology needs to change. Our theology must stop being a root and a support of the cycle of violence. It must begin being a support for the victim and a part of the solution to wife battering.

Theological Reflection

Theology, as a statement of how we understand ourselves in relation to God, draws on the values and images of our culture. In this section we begin to re-examine the traditional language, images, and patterns of thinking of the church, from the perspective of those — especially battered women — who have experienced abuse and victimization. In effect, we are "shifting paradigms," finding the appropriate analogies for our relationship with God. The process may achieve insights; it will certainly contain oversights; but, to serve its purpose, it must of necessity be a continuing enterprise, carried out in and by the Christian community.

1 Women's reality and the Ultimate Reality

This is reality for women in Canada:

> At least one in ten married women in Canada is battered by her husband. . . . The nature of assaults range from a slap on the face to choking . . . to shooting. The Committee has listened to women who have lost teeth, sustained eye injuries and suffered miscarriages as a result of their husbands' attacks. For some victims the psychological abuse following the physical

battering is just as intolerable. (Ontario Standing Committee on Social Development, p. 4)

This section of the paper is an attempt to reflect on the above daily reality of women in Canada in light of the Ultimate Reality we call God. To do so we will explore

a   the pastoral question: To whom can these women and the men who batter them pray?

b   the critical question: In what ways do our images and teachings about God support or invite violence against women? and

c   the hopeful question: What insights of our faith are redemptive in this violent situation?

In many ways these questions will be explored simultaneously so that the questions and their answers will interweave throughout this section.

2 Terror in the Bible

For many battered women their experience of violence at the hands of men is comparable to the social and physical violence experienced by women in the Bible. In her hermeneutical book *Texts of Terror*, Phyllis Trible recounts the lives of Hagar (Gen 21:9–21), Tamar (2 Sam 13:1–22), an unnamed concubine (Judg 19:1–30), and the daughter of Jephthah (Judg 11:29–40). These women are the property and objects of patriarchal lust, hatred, and violence. Fathers, brothers, masters, and strangers are involved in the cruelty that devastates their lives. Terror, isolation, abandonment, mutilation, and even death are their lot. Their stories cry out for the presence of a God who is compassionate and will intercede by defending them and demanding respect for the inviolability and sacredness of their persons. Sadly, the God of Abraham, Isaac, and Jacob is instead silent, absent, or even condoning of the violence in these stories.

Trible warns us that these stories are not "relics of a distant primitive and inferior past . . . history refutes all claims to the superiority of a Christian era" (Trible, p. 2). Nor should the Old Testament God of wrath be put in contrast to the New Testament God of love, since both testaments contain a profound tension between divine wrath and divine love. Moreover, we must not subordinate the suffering of the four women (or any battered woman) to the suffering of the cross for "their passion has its own integrity; no comparisons diminish the terror they knew" (Trible, p. 2). Neither should we gloss over the suffering by promoting the resurrection as the answer to these stories. There can be no answer until the questions inherent in these stories are truly heard.

The terror experienced by the four biblical women parallels the terror of abused women in our own day because "just as art imitates life, scripture likewise reflects it in both its terror and holiness" (Trible, p. 2). Just as the unnamed concubine experienced God's absence/silence in her violent death, so do some women today know only God's absence in the midst of their pain. Just as Jephthah's daughter died as a sacrifice to God in keeping her father's vow (a father who should have protected her), so do some women today know only that the Lord seems to will their suffering at the hands of the man who before God promised to "comfort, honour, and keep her as long as they both shall live." The pain these women experience in being battered is deepened when God is perceived as absent, uncaring or, even worse, condoning the violence which surrounds them (Trible, pp. 1–5).

3) The battered woman's response to God and the church

The experience of being battered has forced many women to ask if they can believe in God when the images for God are male and when a predominantly male church hierarchy seems to be inattentive to their needs. It raises for them serious questions about the absence of an expressed understanding of male domination and battering from the pulpit, from hymns, from prayers, and especially in pastoral care.

> My pastor's reaction was to call and confront me. I hoped for some help, or at least some consolation and advice, but I received only a lecture on having deceived him and the community into thinking we had a Christian marriage. So in my shock and loneliness, I was given no help. In fact my pastor contributed to my isolation and shame. (Anonymous)

The sense of being abandoned by the church experienced by women in battering situations may be reinforced in marriage preparation if no hint is given of the potential for violence in a relationship; in counselling sessions if it is suggested that violence is caused by some behaviour in the victim; or in any pastoral approach that minimizes suffering, that individualizes the problem, or that, passively or actively, upholds the abuser (See Section 10, Domestic ideology and female submission). In the same way, the church needs to beware of any theology that views marriage more as an indissoluble state than as a mutual covenant, or that values the institutions of marriage and family above the quality of relationships within them.

The church's interpretation of key passages which are current in the lectionary and in liturgical usage can also communicate either tolerance for or condemnation of violence in marriage. In this way, for example, the passage in Ephesians 5:21 ff. could be construed as permission for a man to "discipline" and abuse his wife. Or, it could be read as an appeal for husbands and wives to be subject to one another, enjoining the woman to respect her husband, and the man to treat her body as he would his own. Similarly, Luke 17:1-4 contains a statement about repentance and forgiveness that might be confused with superficial notions of remorse and apology that simply perpetuate the cycle of domestic violence. Again, Psalm 55 can be read as a call to endure suffering and abuse, or as an expression of God's compassion for and solidarity with those who suffer needlessly. The standard must be that no reference from scripture can be used to justify the abuse of another human being.

Theological Reflection 39

Thus, the church's teaching about marriage, its use and interpretation of scripture, the pastoral care shown by clergy and congregations, and the awareness of women's issues combine to make clear, strong statements to the battered woman, and will influence her faith development and her decision to leave or to stay with her faith community.

While there are those who have stayed in communion with the church and continue to struggle for meaning within the Christian framework, there are many who have lost all sense of a loving God and simply try to survive within a society of violence.

> I was abused by my mother and father. I'd lived it all my life. So when my husband abused me then left me, I just thought, "Oh, you know, it's just part of it, well, society's way of doing things. It was just the usual set-up. (Anonymous)

For some, God has abandoned them. For others, God is the source of authority behind the male authority who beats them. For others, God seems as violent as the violence with which they live. All of these women need to be heard by the church.

4 Hearing vulnerability

It is not easy for the church to hear these women or to accept their experience. Yet Jesus made special reference in his teaching to those who, like these women, were vulnerable and lacking in status and position. The term *mikros** — "the least" or "the lesser ones" — attributed to Jesus in the New Testament, was used to include all who were powerless or marginalized within society. Jesus placed the "lesser ones" firmly at the centre of the kingdom, giving them claim to the same spiritual dignity as prophets and righteous men. By doing this, by speaking of his own disciples as "the lesser ones" (Mt 10:40–42; Mk 9:42), he deeply challenged contemporary assumptions about power and greatness.

> The question of greatness took on great significance because the striving to be great permeated all Palestinian piety. On all occasions, at worship, at court, in common meals, in every

affair, the question constantly arose who was the greater, and according to each his due honour was an important matter which caused constant concern. By breaking the disciples free from this tradition Jesus gave His community a completely new form.*

Yet the church has not been completely faithful to Jesus' radical teaching about greatness. Much in our theology and institutional structure reinforces a belief in a hierarchy of male dominance, a belief which contributes towards the tolerance for and practice of violence against women. We need to recover a theology which values the "lesser ones" whom others exploit or disregard, and which reaches to the victim rather than the victor.

Why? The nature of violence is that it is both hierarchical and cyclical. This is why it is successful in its terrorizing and long-term control of its victims. Violence is hierarchical in that for someone to be violently in control and dominant, someone else must be battered (physically and psychologically) and submissive (Fortune, p. 18). In domestic situations, the victims are usually women and children. Violence is cyclical in that, more often than not, it breeds more violence. For children, the dominance/submission pattern is reinforced early in life, both in violent homes and through society's norms in general (Ontario Standing Committee, pp. 2–3).

Yet all too often we teach our children to respond differently to violence on the basis of gender. In our society we teach the boy child to use his aggression against others in order to define himself as "a man" (Toch, 1969), while at the same time we teach the girl child to suppress her aggression in the service of others. From this, it is possible to conclude that men raised to be violently aggressive more readily commit homicidal acts such as battering,

---

mikros is sometimes translated as "little ones," a term which, in this context, has the disadvantage of evoking a condescending attitude which has existed about women. At the same time, it does convey the powerlessness and disfranchisement experienced by many women. For the source of the quotation above, see *mikros* in G. Kittel (ed.), *Theological Dictionary of the New Testament* (Grand Rapids, Michigan: W.B. Eerdmans, 1967), vol. IV, especially p. 655, footnote 33, quotation from A. Schlatter in *Die Kirche des Matthäus* (Gütersloh, 1929), p. 543.

while women raised to deny aggression are more readily passive in the face of violence against them. (See Section 9, Domestic hierarchy, tension management, and control of wives, for Lenore Walker's use of "learned helplessness" to describe this sydrome.) The two gender-taught responses intersect to perpetuate violence (Ontario Standing Committee, p. 3).

The church's call to renounce violence as abhorrent to the Christian understanding of "family" and "home" must include an acknowledgement of its own participation, through its theology, in a pattern of dominance and submission. Using this theology the church has expressed its abhorrence of violence, on the one hand, while teaching a hierarchical understanding of authority and power that contributes to violence, on the other. Where, in all of this, is Jesus' teaching about the "lesser ones"? How sensitive are we to hearing vulnerability?

5 Towards a theology which reaches out to the victim

We might characterize a theology which supports dominance as a theology which reaches out to the victor. Through a series of questions we will explore the victor theology and at the same time try to outline a theology which reaches out to the victim.

a What does it mean to be human?

A victor theology is one which emphasizes the division of humanity into differences, into male and female, into greater and lesser. Moreover, greater is better than lesser, male is better than female. Throughout the life of the church there have been many who have taught that to be male is to be closer to (the male) God than the female is. Thomas Aquinas taught, for example, that the male fetus received his soul at an earlier age than the female. Males were spiritually privileged.

While the church today may have abandoned such explicit teachings, there are still residues of them in our theology. Take, for example, the language of the Creed which even in the ICET revision translates the words of incarnation as "Christ became man" rather than "Christ became human" or "Christ became one of us" (*Prayers We Have in Common*, p. 11). This is more important than we may at first realize because if, ultimately, Christ's maleness is made sacred to his power, then women are inevitably cast as the other, the less-than-perfect, the power-less. And when one person is assumed to be less than the other — when femaleness is assumed to be less than maleness — a relationship of dominance and submission results: a power struggle more concerned with violence than compassion, more concerned with maintaining negative power than being mutually creative while exercising mutual power.

For men and women to be mutually creative suggests that there must be a mutual vulnerability to one another as persons. The sexuality or gender of a person becomes then a gift the person brings to relationships and to the world, but it is only one aspect of the value of that person. To be human is to be created in the image of God. "Male and female God created them" (Gen 1:27).

b   What images do we have for God?
Central to the Christian image of God is the understanding of God as the Trinity — Father, Son, and Holy Ghost. The language of the Trinity, as the church has reinforced it, is essentially hierarchical, static, and discrete. "Father," "Son," and "Holy Ghost" may have originated as images of a living, personal God; but by usage and connotation, they now convey the opposite. In a patriarchal society, "Father" has come to be associated with a role of authority, power, and control; "Son" has become a term of gender (male offspring) rather than relationship (child of love); and "Holy Ghost" comes from the vocabulary of another age, and has lost its root meaning. The result is an image of God that is static, detached from creation, and non-nurturing.

The doctrine of the Trinity has often been used to reinforce the value of a hierarchical order of creation. In this view, hierarchy, as long as it is understood as the sacred rule of a loving and benevolent Father-God, is good and necessary for giving order and control to unruly forces. The dilemma is that if hierarchy is understood as the sacred rule of anyone who is a "father-figure," it can reinforce a belief that the male has the right to discipline his unruly wife and children — by force if necessary. Indeed, as we have seen (Section 5, Ideological aspects), the church has historically supported men who physically punished their wives.

If our images for God, such as Father-God or Lord and King, are exclusively male, the woman battered by her husband, or the child abused by a father or father-figure, may have no means for perceiving God as loving and protective of the vulnerable.

The disparity between image and experience, and the delicate issue of language about God, is powerfully illustrated in this anonymous prayer-poem, written from the perspective of children who have experienced "father" as abusive, distant, and untrustworthy.

The Lord's Prayer

Our Father
This is us three kids talking to you.
Who art in heaven
You're so distant and so aloof. It seems like nothing touches you.
And every day you go off to work someplace, you're never around.
Hallowed be thy name
And yet, boy, do we ever feel your presence. Everything is done
in your name. "Wait till your father gets home." We know what
you will allow or what you demand. You don't even have to be
there to tell us.
Thy kingdom come
You want us to
Thy will be done
do everything you say
On earth
at home
As it is in heaven.
just like they do at the office.
Give us this day
Can we have some money
Our daily bread
to buy lunch?
And forgive our debt
Why can't you be as understanding
As we forgive our debtors.
as our friends?
And lead us not
Oh, please don't make me do it,

Into temptation
  not again.
But deliver us
  It's my fault.
From evil.
  I'm the guilty one.
For thine
  You decide,
Is the kingdom
  you name,
and the power
  you take,
and the glory
  you destroy,
Forever.
  always.
AMEN*

What does it mean for such children to "obey the Father," or for a battered wife to "listen to her Lord"? What lifelong impact do these images have on abused children who grow up to be parents or spouses who continue the violent cycle, either as abusers or as victims?

Some would say that using languages and images that include the stories and experiences of women is the real answer for allowing the battered woman or abused child to speak freely to God, within her or his own pain, in prayer, and in worship. Yet we must be careful about insisting that God as Mother, for example, will bring healing to the battered person. The following letter suggests that for one abused child, now an adult, no such comfort is found.

I have not yet confronted my father for his incest of me. I am afraid. He is still all-powerful to me. And I realized at five that God the Father and father the god were one and the same. I knew what God did. He would find you no matter where you were and he made you do unspeakable things and you

*Poem distributed at National Conference on Family Violence, led by Marie Fortune in San Antonio, Texas, March, 1985.

could never stop him because he was all-powerful and all-present, and you could never tell anybody because who could you tell on God? Nobody was bigger than he was. *God the Mother*? I knew that was a lie. She wasn't as big as he was, and she was scared of him just like I was. She was scared to stand up to him, so she didn't protect me from him. The Son? He did to me what the father did. I knew he was just like the father, and would grow up to be god too. (Anonymous)

In any case, the exclusive nature of the church's language, and the prevailing use of male and power images for God, such as Father Almighty, King, Lord of Hosts, have had the effect of marginalizing or excluding the pain and life perceptions of battered women from worship and story-telling. Excluded also are the men and women who are lost in their own abuse of power and do not know how to be other than all-powerful themselves. There are no alternatives given for them either.

Some would advocate changing the personal language of Father-Son-Spirit to the image of an active God who initiates life (Creator), who continually gives life (Sustainer), and who transforms death into life (Sanctifier). Such a paradigm of God invites us to explore partnership with, rather than control over, others. Yet here too there are limitations. Such language describes God in terms of function or position and diminishes the Christian insight that God is deeply personal.

What then shall we do? The Christian community is called at this time to struggle with the language and images we use for God so that both the deeply personal "Abba" (upon whom Jesus called) and the community-in-love (which is the Trinity) are upheld in ways that do not exclude the insights and perceptions of those people caught in domestic violence. We need to find new ways of acknowledging that for some of us God is the Absent One, the Silent One, the Wrathful One. Perhaps it is when we allow such painful images of God to enter our corporate life that we will be free to discover God anew.

c Who is Christ?
A theology which emphasizes Christ as Victor, at the expense of Christ as Victim, is in danger of becoming a teaching which reaches out to the victor rather than the victim in society.

One classic work which sets forth Christ as Victor is Gustav Aulen's *Christus Victor*. In this book, Aulen attempts to re-work a theology of the atonement which goes beyond "objective" theories that make God the *object* of Christ's atoning work, reconciled to humanity by the satisfaction of justice, or the "subjective" theories that recognize the work of the atonement as a subjective change essentially taking place in individual people, not a change in attitude on the part of God towards humanity. Aulen tries to develop a theology which understands the atoning work of Christ as a conflict with, and victory over, the powers of evil, that ultimately, in the resurrection, brings about a radical new relationship between God and the world.

However, a simplistic version of this theology could be used inappropriately to suggest that, just as Christ the (male) Son and King becomes the Victor, so the sons of men are entitled to reign as victors in their domain. And if the reasoning is that "a man's home is his castle," then (as "king") he is entitled to rule over its occupants.

The point is not to deny that Christ was victorious over the powers of evil, but to remember that Christ is first made known to the "lesser ones" as the victim, the one who cried from the cross, "My God, my God, why have you forsaken me?" It is in recognizing Christ as the abandoned victim of violence that we begin to apprehend God as the Helpless One.

Christ the Victim is the one who freely emptied himself to become the servant of all. Here, it is important to understand clearly the nature of the suffering and victimization of Christ. Jesus' voluntary suffering and death on the cross cannot and must not be paralleled with the involuntary suffering of women, children, or other victims of violence, nor be used to justify their situation in any way. Marie Fortune makes an emphatic distinction between voluntary and involuntary suffering:

> *Voluntary suffering* is a painful experience which a person chooses in order to accomplish a greater good. For example, the acts of civil disobedience by civil rights workers in the United States in the 1960's led to police brutality and imprisonment. These consequences were unjustifiable and should not have been inflicted. Yet people chose to endure this suffering

in order to change the circumstances of oppression which caused even greater suffering for many people. Like voluntary suffering, *involuntary suffering* is unjustifiable in any circumstances; it should never happen. However, unlike voluntary suffering, involuntary suffering is not chosen and serves no greater good. Rape and child sexual abuse are forms of involuntary suffering. Neither serves any useful purpose; neither is chosen by the victim, neither should ever happen to anyone. Yet both do happen. (Fortune, p. 196–7)

This distinction has serious implications for a proper theology of the cross and resurrection. Jesus was not sent to the cross by God for punishment, nor to test his faith, nor to build character. Jesus was made a victim of violence at the hands of the Romans in a devastating, meaningless act of brutality which left him feeling abandoned and betrayed, and his friends in despair. The resurrection was the radical and surprising realization that God can be present even in such an event, that suffering can be redeemed, and that the possibility of new life can arise even from such meaninglessness and suffering. The resurrection was not a retrospective justification for the cross, nor a reason for minimizing any human experience of pain or helplessness. As Marie Fortune continues,

Sometimes Jesus' crucifixion is misinterpreted as being the model for suffering. Since Jesus went to the cross, according to the interpretation, persons should bear their own crosses of irrational violence (e.g. rape) without complaint. Rather than the sanctification of suffering, Jesus' crucifixion remains a witness to the horror of violence. It is not a model of how suffering should be borne, but a witness to God's desire that no one should have to suffer such violence again. (Fortune, p. 198)

The pastoral implications are no less significant. Suffering of any kind must be recognized as contrary to God's will for humanity, and its victims must be upheld in their search for safety and freedom. Fortune points out that

In this sense, experience of suffering . . . present a victim with
an occasion for new life, i.e. the occasion of becoming a sur-
vivor. . . . Whether or not the experience of life indeed
becomes this depends largely on the kind of response that the
victim receives from family, friends, the Church, and other
institutions she/he may encounter. A supportive response will
maximize the possibility for healing; a non-supportive response
will, to a large degree, eliminate such a possibility. (Fortune,
p. 198)

The honouring of Christ as Victim helps us to honour those
who are victims in our society. All too often in the church our
discomfort with pain and helplessness causes us to minimize the
victimization of Jesus in order to glory in Christ the Victor. Both
truths about Christ need to be held together if we are to stand
with the victims of our time on the one hand, and, on the other
hand, to declare to the ''great ones'' and winners of our society,
that their dominating victory is *not* the victory of Christ.

d   Who is Mary?

The traditional picture of Mary is one which portrays her as the
pure and submissive virgin and mother. Her obedience to God
is seen as her submission to and passive acceptance of God's will.
This image of Mary reinforces the belief that women, following
her example, should obey God by being submissively obedient.
Indeed, women have been counselled to stay in abusive situations and emulate Mary's obedient passivity.

This view of Mary, however, diminishes her. A richer picture
of Mary is one which sees her as actively cooperating with the
God of Life. Mary's aggressive decision to conceive without
asking Joseph's permission, her willingness to say ''yes'' even
though her political position as a woman put her at risk, exem-
plifies this active role. Here we see an assertive, independent,
courageous person of passion and faith. The battered woman
whose learned paralysis has become a prison can find in such
a Mary an impetus to action.

e   What is sin?

Our teaching about sin has also been rooted in the value system
and experience of the victors. Sin is generally understood to mean

the misuse of power, usually by individuals, sometimes by groups, over people and things. This kind of thinking reinforces the hidden value, that it is *appropriate* to use power over people and things as long as it is "responsibly" used. The problem with this understanding of sin is that it excludes those without power, those in the submissive position. How can the "seven cardinal sins" — pride, anger, envy, covetousness, gluttony, lust, and sloth — be related to victims of physical or psychological violence, or economic or political exploitation? The absurd result is that people who are treated as worthless, and already experience themselves as such, find themselves apologizing for their anger and confessing their "unworthiness" or "wickedness" Sunday after Sunday.

The church needs to explore what it means to describe sin differently. What would happen if sin were seen as indifference towards oneself and one's degradation rather than pride or lust; as acceptance of violence or the refusal to react rather than anger or sloth? When sin is redefined and penance is seen as working to restore justice, then the cycle of violence may be broken.

f What is the church?

The models of authority in the church also have the capacity to support the victor or the "little ones." There is much in the history of the church which reinforces a belief that certain groups of people have "power over" others. Yet there is also within our history an understanding of the church as a transformed and transforming body of people — the servant community.

If we see the church as God's family in the sense that it is a place where one can be honoured and nurtured, then we are free to insist that the human family unit, to be truly family, also needs to be a place where one is honoured, nurtured, and therefore safe. The family unit should not be elevated to a sacrosanct position in society thereby excluding other nurturing groupings. The true family and the true church are where the little ones are heard and healed and honoured.

6 Summary

At the beginning of this section we said we would raise some questions and sketch some answers with regard to the way our theology reinforces violence against women. What we have done is a beginning but no more than that. There is much yet to be done if we are to break the cycle of violence. Let us work to make a theology which reaches out to the victim — a theology which is firmly on the agenda of the church.

Response Strategies for the Church

1 Re-visioning hidden traditions and images

The church must respond to the victimization of and violence against women within society of which it is becoming increasingly aware, as well as to its own complicity in such abusive "power over" within its own theology and practice. The response needed is a major project of revision, but it is also a manageable project in that there are a good number of specific issues on which the church might move. The specific issues will obviously be those which suggest the most immediate remedy, but the more important long-term changes will never take place unless the major re-visioning is always sought. Continual rethinking as to the nature and role of women and men within society and the church must always remain the *rationale* which provides incentive to address any immediate issue or practice.

In this paper we have been outlining the sociological, economic, and cultural analyses which provide sufficient understandings as to why and where such violence takes place. The theological reflection has probed the church's heritage in theology and practice which has both reinforced and critiqued such social and cultural violence against women. The dominant metaphor which has emerged is that of wife and woman as *victim* in both a Jewish and a Christian social structure where the real focus has typically been the *victor* — in God, in Christ, in *man*kind. Yet current scholarship in biblical and historical fields is increasingly showing evidence of other "forgotten" and "hidden" traditions of women as well as men significantly involved in the acts of salvation, and those acts are understood not only as "victories" but also as births, gifts, transformations, and other more humane metaphors. We are convinced that the church must become active and committed to a recovery of these traditions and memories not only in its schools of theology, but also in the theology by which it *lives* — in decision making, in liturgy, in understanding the gospel in our times. This will be neither simple nor painless. Theology and liturgy attentive to victims and victimization cannot be developed and led by those who have known mostly success, privilege, and power in church and society — our current "victors." As Christ willingly became victim, so the church must follow the way of the cross. It must become intimately involved with and aware of the phenomenon of victimization and violence which results from the pursuit of greatness which is no respecter of persons.

In Canadian society, there are many victims — and they are by no means only women. But women abused in their homes, overlooked in their jobs, invisible in leadership, and alone in their fear, are among those who can share their concern about addressing the God for whom they yearn as "King," "Almighty," "Victorious," and one of "power and might." Did not this God eternally take on the identity of all the abused and victimized in history at Golgotha, for the church to raise up the mark of abuse, the cross, as the incarnate meaning of God's redemption in Jesus? This awareness of the constant victimization and abuse of persons in history must be re-discovered in the life and liturgy of the church, not only for all of womankind, but for all of humankind!

2 Alternatives which humanize economic, political and social relationships

Just as devotional life and liturgy can be transformed by the recovery of theological traditions by which God shares in and brings meaning to human victimization, so single, family, and community life can be transformed by the recovery of alternate social, economic, and political relationships which promote partnership, cooperation, and mutual commitment rather than dominance, violence, and submission. The church has only cosmetically critiqued the Roman patriarchal system which it took on when, in the fourth century, it became the Roman church victorious rather than an association of culturally differing Christian communities persecuted. There had been scarcely two centuries of experiencing the generosity in worth and value of the early Christian communities, which manifests itself when persecution and victimization make clear a real equality between Jew and Greek, slave and free, male and female. It is precisely this generosity of spirit which third world Christian communities, who experience real abuse and victimization in these times, are attempting to export back to the first world as the real meaning of spiritually reborn communities.

If the church were promoting such images of relational worth and value, it would be finally putting aside cultural memories of domination with men as "king of the castle," women and children as acquired property to be possessed, and the family as a society in miniature to be ruled. Women and children would not be the only ones to benefit, but so would men themselves, as responsibility and support became shared rather than projected on any *one*. This would, of course, model a different mode of economic, political, and social relating as well as affecting domestic life. Power, gained, withheld, or lost would soon evidence itself as insufficient for all economic and political decision-making. Other more sensitive and relational metaphors would emerge. The church's promotion of such humanized domestic and ecclesial living would surely open up possibilities for Christ's humanization of social, political, and economic living as well.

Such recovery and revisioning of the nature of our relationship with God in faith and life, as well as our practice of it in domestic and social living, is a very broad undertaking indeed. Yet we would identify it as the necessary and motivating recovery which must be a part of dealing with any *particular* issue of abuse. But even with the limited analysis and reflection of this paper, there are several areas that we would identify for immediate consideration.

3 The language of liturgy and sacrament

Within the life and liturgy of the church, we welcome enthusiastically the care taken in the Canadian *Book of Alternative Services* to increase significantly the accessability of the images of God and humankind to men and women alike. Some thought has also been given to titles as well as to images of authority, and these are all helpful. We would hope that still further revision in this direction would take place before the book's acceptance, since what is abusive in language and liturgy is very much a current and emergent discovery. While that book is and will be a helpful alternative, there remain the language and practice of the current Prayer Book. We would urge that the Doctrine and Worship Committee identify particularly abusive prayers and practices — such as the patriarchal ''giving'' of the woman by the father in the marriage service — and suggest alternatives which retain the language but not the abuse. This will doubtless be seen as divisive by some, but surely there are limits even to ''Anglican comprehensiveness'' when it comes to what we *now* understand to be language and practices which promote abuse and violation of persons.

4 Prophetic about human partnership

Not only for the life of its members, but also for the exemplary effect upon society, the church must pay particular attention to its preparation, education, support, and pastoral counselling for marriage and raising children. The family unit has the effect of being a microcosm of society, and all too often the abuses here are *only* dealt with when they happen to come into public view. Marriage preparation has been an excellent practice to begin a process of education for marriage, but it is time that it function not merely as a *preventative* for marital problems but rather as *prophetic* to a transformed understanding of human partnership. The co-creativeness of God and humankind, woman and man, parents and children, needs to be raised up and advocated. This should continue in the preaching, teaching, and community life of the church, which must hold up the nature of partnership while admitting that the signs of brokenness in violence, abuse, and neglect *are* prevalent in our society, particularly given the economic and social presures exerted by systems which have little respect for persons.

5 Advocacy and education

Neither women, nor anyone else, should be "assigned" to manage and/or internalize the tension that contemporary capitalism inflicts upon its workers. This the "system" must manage. And finally, without disgrace, those struggling in abusing families and marriages should be able to receive pastoral care, protection, and support without stigma or the projection of guilt that they have failed the norm of Christian marriage. In the community, the church can do much in this area. Advocacy for equality in property and assets is an important issue in current divorce practices. Education in community on the reality of domestic violence is important so that the community and law enforcement agencies take the matter seriously, rather than continue the current "hands off" approach.

Just as child abuse registries are kept, so could wife abuse registries be kept — this is at least one way of trying to halt the perpetuation of abuse. Perhaps particularly within society at large, the church, which once encouraged the beating of one's wife out of "charity and concern for her soul," should face squarely the sinfulness of that tradition by acknowledging that in current marriages the victims are clearly the wives, and that the beatings must stop for the sake of *all* their souls!

As we as a taskforce have studied violence against women, we have consistently found that the *source* of the violence is seldom if ever one issue, group, or institution. Rather it is typically a series of what we have called *"mutually reinforcing systems and hierarchies,"* which promote divisions within humanity of those deemed greater and those deemed lesser. That many are deemed lesser means many become exploited, abused, and victimized by society and institutions. These institutions include the church. But our analysis consistently shows that many, if not most, of those deemed lesser are women — wives, ex-wives, and other single women. Our economic system exploits them. Our political system tries to ignore them. Our church life uses yet seldom recognizes them. Our theological understandings seem to have forgotten identification of them as the victims within our midst. And even if that identification were made, in liturgy and living we seem to have forgotten that we and Jesus the Christ took on incarnate victimization itself, and singled it out as that area of human life most in need of redemption. Yet the gospel remains inextricably linked to that struggle for life and worth out of victimization and violation. So long as we sense violation — in this case the violation of women within both church and society — we sense that plight of humanity which God in Christ met in the redemption of Jesus for all of humanity. Being faithful in recollection and remembrance to this act of God will bring both revision and transformation of our current beliefs, understandings, and practices so that we may once again and over again find our place with the "little ones," the neglected ones, the victims in our midst — and uplift the worth, value, and life of even the "least of these."

Appendix

Act 27 of General Synod 1983 and Recommendations for Action

At Fredericton, New Brunswick, in June 1983 the General Synod of the Anglican Church of Canada passed the following resolution:

THAT the General Synod request every diocese and parish to commit itself to using its own resources and to working with community groups to eliminate family violence and especially, in focusing on the battering of women, to engage in the following areas for action:

1 to declare publicly that the violence is wrong and that it must stop;

2 to support the emergency and longer-term services necessary to protect battered women and to enable them to re-establish their lives;

3 to lobby, where necessary, for changes in law, and in police, court, and social service procedures to ensure that women and men are treated justly;

4 to undertake preventive work in the areas of marriage preparation and family life by exploring the issues related to wife-battering,

e.g. isolation and dependence for the wife, and the husband's authority over his wife;

5 to provide further education for the clergy and laity in their roles as counsellors in this area.

The passing of Act 27 above was an important milestone for the church; with this action the issue of family violence became part of the official agenda of the Anglican Church of Canada in terms both of ministry and of mission. The issue was no longer seen as the concern only of a few small groups like the Women's Unit's Taskforce on Violence against Women; at General Synod representatives of the whole church — men and women, clergy and lay, young and old — took the first steps in understanding the "mutually reinforcing hierarchies" which foster and perpetuate the physical and emotional abuse of women by their partners. On behalf of the whole church, the members of General Synod also committed themselves, in a general way, to a course of public lobbying for improvements in legislation and services and to education on this issue within the church community.

In response to Act 27 of General Synod 1983, therefore, and in an effort to assist the Anglican Church of Canada in its commitment to address the issue of domestic violence against women, we offer the following recommendations:

1 That *congregations* devote the penitential seasons of Lent or Advent to a comprehensive study program in the area of family violence, with an initial focus on wife assault. Parish groups will find it most helpful to examine their local situations, investigating the following areas: what wife assault is (a criminal assault) and is not (the act of a mentally-ill man, deserved or enjoyed by the wife); police attitudes and procedure for handling domestic assaults; emergency resources for women who wish to leave a battering situation — shelters, safe houses, children's programs, legal assistance available to battered women, status of provincial legislation relating to wife assault; the church's complicity in fostering a cultural climate in which domestic assaults on women are largely overlooked; and the church's potential as an agent for change. A variety of educational strategies should be used: sermons, Bible study, assigned reading, speakers from the community, films, discussion groups.

As members of the congregation become educated in this area, they may wish to become more action-oriented and to lobby for change in church and community; indeed, such action by church people is at least one of the goals of congregational education. Group members may also wish to broaden the scope of their concern to include other forms of violence against women (rape, pornography) or other forms of family violence (child sexual and physical abuse, abuse of dependent elderly).

One word of caution, however: the Taskforce on Violence against Women has observed a tendency within the church to understand the issue of wife assault as a "women's problem." Many, therefore, expect that those most interested in parish study and action groups on this subject will be women, and initially this may well be the case. Parish leaders, clergy and lay, need to be aware of this dynamic and be prepared to give strong encouragement to members of parish councils, human rights groups, social action, outreach, and Christian Education committees to see this issue as a problem for the *whole* church which requires the response of the whole church.

2 That *parish, diocesan, and national marriage and family-life educators* undertake a critical review of curriculum materials currently used in the church for marriage preparation, marriage enrichment, and parenting courses, bearing in mind the following questions: What kinds of messages about what it means to be male and female are we communicating in this course? Are we contributing, indirectly through sex-role stereotyping or in a more overt way through the use of materials which understand violence as a form of "discipline," to the problem of family violence? Are we teaching men and women that while anger and conflict are inevitable in any relationship, violence is not? Do we raise the question of marital violence explicitly in our marriage preparation courses, communicating clearly that violence is unacceptable behaviour and preparing young people to deal with it appropriately if it happens? Are we raising the question of corporal punishment (which models the use of physical force as a solution to family disagreement) in parenting classes? Are we teaching people of all ages non-violent communication techniques? Curriculum materials which stereotype or which do not explicitly raise the issue of family violence must be amended appropriately or dropped from use.

3   That *parish, diocesan, and national social action staff and volunteers* critically evaluate the legislation and legal practices in their area in light of the following considerations: Wife battering is a violent crime and should always be treated as an assault. Further, it is the perpetrator of the assault, and not the victim, who is on trial throughout the legal proceedings. The attitudes of judges and lawyers, as well as the content of legislation, need to be monitored and challenged on an ongoing basis.

4   That *theological educators and others responsible for the formation of clergy in Anglican colleges in Canada* provide education about family violence and skill training in dealing with the violent family as a mandatory component of education for ministry.

5   That *bishops and diocesan program staff* provide mandatory, episcopally endorsed training events for the clergy of each diocese on pastoral and educational strategies for dealing with family violence.

6   That *bishops, personnel officers, and others having a concern for clergy family life* recognize that wife assault is a problem in clergy families as it is in all other sectors of the population, and develop strategies for responding to the special concerns and needs of battered clergy wives and abusive male clergy.

Space limitations preclude an exhaustive list of available resources and possible program designs for the various kinds of education recommended above. Over the past five years, members of the Taskforce on Violence against Women have developed considerable expertise in program planning and would be pleased to consult with interested groups as time and funding constraints allow. We may be contacted through:

The Taskforce on Violence against Women
c/o Jeanne Rowles
Anglican Church of Canada
600 Jarvis Street
Toronto, Ontario M4Y 2J6
(416) 924-9192

Bibliography
of Works Cited

Adams, David C. and McCormick, Andrew J. "Men unlearning violence: a group approached based on the collective model," pp. 170–197 in Maria Roy, ed., *The Abusive Partner: An Analysis of Domestic Battering*. New York: Van Nostrand Reinhold, 1982.

Alsdurf, Jim M. "Wife Abuse and the Church: the Response of Pastors." *Response* Winter 8(2) (1985), 9–11.

Baker, Elizabeth F. *Technology and Women's Work*. New York: Columbia University, 1964.

Bauer, Carol and Ritt, Lawrence. "'A Husband is a Beating Animal': Frances Power Cobbe confronts the wife-abuse problem in Victorian England." *International Journal of Women's Studies* 6(2) (1983), 99–118.

Brand, Johanna. "Loved, Honoured and Bruised" pamphlet, National Film Board of Canada, 1980.

Davidson, Terry. *Conjugal Crime*. New York: Ballantine Books, 1978.

Dobash R.P. and R.E. Dobash. *Violence Against Wives: A Case Against the Patriarchy*. New York: Free Press, 1979.

Eberts, Mary. "The Person's Case," *Status of Women News* Vol. 5, no. 3, March 1979, 16–18.

Falk, Gail. "Women and Unions: A Historical View," mimeographed, New Haven, Connecticut: Yale Law School, 1970 (cited by Hartmann, 1976, p. 163).

Fawcett, Millicent G. Review of *Women in the Printing Trades,* ed. J. Ramsay MacDonald, *Economic Journal* 14 (2) June 1904, 295–99.

Finch, Janet. *Married to the Job: Wives' Incorporation in Men's Work.* London: George Allen and Unwin, 1983.

Fiorenza, Elizabeth Schussler. *In Memory of Her.* New York: Crossroad, 1983.

Fortune, Marie and Denise Hormann. *Family Violence: A Workshop Manual for Rural Communities.* Seattle, Washington: The Center for the Prevention of Sexual and Domestic Violence, 1980.

Fortune, Marie. "The Church and Domestic Violence," *Theology. News and Notes,* Fuller Theological Seminary Alumni, 1982, 17–21.

Fox, Bonnie, ed. *Hidden in the Household: Women's Domestic Labour Under Capitalism.* Toronto: The Women's Press, 1980.

Gage, Matilda Joslyn. *Woman, Church and State: The Original Expose of Male Collaboration Against the Female Sex.* Watertown, Mass.: Persephone Press, 1893 (reprinted 1980).

Gaguin, Deirdre A. "Spouse abuse: data from the National Crime Survey," *Victimology* 2, (3–4) (1977–78), 643–647.

Hall, Catherine. "The Early Formation of Victorian Domestic Ideology." In *Fit Work for Women,* edited by Sandra Burman. London: Croom Helm, 1979.

Hartman, Heidi. "Capitalism, Patriarchy and Job Segregation by Sex," *Signs* I (3), 1976, pt. 2, 137–169.

Killoran, M. Maureen. "All in a Day's Work: Wife Abuse and Domestic Labour in Contemporary Canadian Society." Paper presented at C.S.S.A. annual meeting, Ottawa, June 1982. Mimeographed.

Luxton, Meg. *More Than a Labour of Love.* Toronto: Women's Press, 1980.

MacLeod, Linda. *Wife Battering in Canada: The Vicious Circle.* Ottawa: Canadian Advisory Council on the Status of Women, 1980.

Meissner, Martin et al. "No Exit for Wives: Sexual Division of Labour and the Cumulation of Household Demands." *Canadian Review of Sociology and Anthropology* 12:424–439.

National Council of Welfare. *Poverty on the Increase.* Ottawa: Department of Health and Welfare, 1985.

Ontario Standing Committee on Social Development. *First Report on Violence: Wife Battering.* Toronto: Queen's Park, 1983.

Prayers We Have in Common: Agreed Liturgical Texts proposed by the International Consultation on English Texts (London: Geoffrey Chapman, 1971).

Raimondi, Norma. "Sexual Division of Labour: What Wives and Husbands Do At Home." Master's Thesis, Department of Sociology, University of Saskatchewan, 1983.

Roy, Maria, ed. *The Abusive Partner: An Analysis of Domestic Battering.* New York: Van Nostrand Reinhold, 1982.

Ruether, Rosemary. "The Cult of True Womanhood." *Commonweal* 99, November 9, 1973, 127–132.

Schewendinger, Julia R. and Schewendinger, Herman. *Rape and Inequality.* Beverley Hills: Sage Publications, 1983.

Seeley, John R.; Sim, R.A.; and Loosley, E.W. *Crestwood Heights: A Study of the Culture of Suburban Life.* 1963. New York: Science Editions, Wiley, 1963.

Smith, Dorothy E. "The Ideological Practice of Sociology." *Catalyst* 8, Winter 1974, 39–54.

Smith, Dorothy E. "Women, the Family, and Corporate Capitalism." In *Women in Canada,* edited by M. Stephenson, pp. 14–18. Don Mills: General Publishing, 1977.

Smith, Dorothy E. "Women, Class and Family." Paper prepared for Social Sciences and Humanities' Research Council Workshop on Women and the Canadian Labour Force, 2–4 October 1980, at University of British Columbia. Mimeographed.

Stark-Adamec, Cannie, and Adamec, Robert E. "Aggression in Men Against Women: Adaptation or Aberration?" *International Journal of Women's Studies* 5(1), Jan-Feb 1982, 1–21.

Storrie, Kathleen. "Woman-Battering and the Anglican Church of Canada." Address given to the General Synod, Anglican Church of Canada, 7 June 1983, at Fredericton. Mimeographed.

Storrie, Kathleen. "Wife Abuse and the Criminal Justice System." Paper presented at the annual meeting of the Western Association of Sociology and Anthropology, 1985, in Winnipeg. Mimeographed.

Swidler, Leonard. *Biblical Affirmation of Women.* Philadelphia: The Westminster Press, 1979.

Tavard, George H. *Woman in Christian Tradition.* Notre Dame: University of Notre Dame Press, 1973.

Trible, Phyllis. *Texts of Terror.* Philadelphia: Fortress Press, 1984.

Walker, Lenore E. "Battered Women and Learned Helplessness." *Victimology* 8 (1–2), 82–104.

Walker, Lenore E. *The Battered Woman.* New York: Harper and Row, 1979.

Women's Bureau. *Women in the Labour Force: Part II — Earnings.* Ottawa: Labour Canada, 1984.